Contents

What are pulleys and gears?

Pulleys and gears are special wheels. They help to make some machines move.

When you turn the crank handle on this model windmill, it makes the sails turn. The handle and the sails are linked by a rubber band. This is the **drive belt**. The drive belt is stretched over two pulleys. It makes both pulleys turn together.

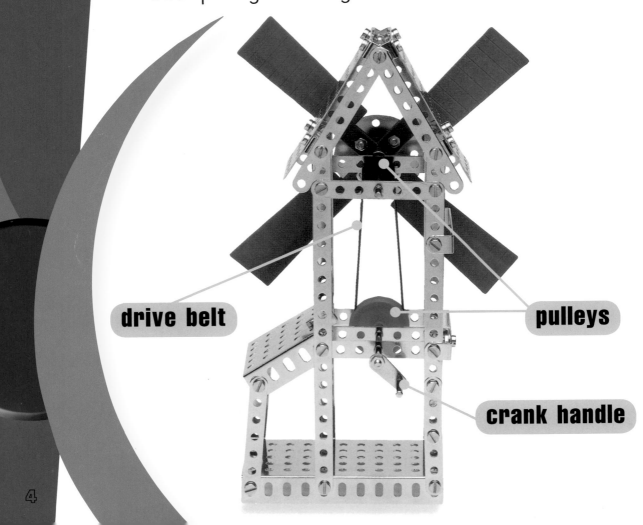

drive belt

pulleys

crank handle

What Do PULLEYS AND GEARS Do?

Heinemann
LIBRARY

David Glover

www.heinemann.co.uk/library
Visit our website to find out more information about Heinemann Library books.

To order:
 Phone 44 (0) 1865 888066
Send a fax to 44 (0) 1865 314091
 Visit the Heinemann Bookshop at www.heinemann.co.uk/library to browse our catalogue and order online.

First published in Great Britain by Heinemann Library, Halley Court, Jordan Hill, Oxford OX2 8EJ, part of Harcourt Education. Heinemann is a registered trademark of Harcourt Education Ltd.

© Harcourt Education Ltd 1996, 2006
Second edition first published in paperback in 2007
The moral right of the proprietor has been asserted.

Editorial: Clare Lewis and Katie Shepherd
Design: Victoria Bevan and Q2A Creative
Illustrations: Barry Atkinson (pp5, 17, 21), Douglas Hall (p6) and Tony Kenyon (p4)
Picture Research: Mica Brancic
Production: Helen McCreath
Printed and bound in China by WKT Company Limited

13 digit ISBN 978 0 431 06407 9 (hardback)
10 digit ISBN 0 431 06407 5 (hardback)
10 09 08 07 06
10 9 8 7 6 5 4 3 2 1

13 digit ISBN 978 0 431 06420 8 (paperback)
10 digit ISBN 0 431 06420 2 (paperback)
11 10 09 08 07
10 9 8 7 6 5 4 3 2 1

British Library Cataloguing in Publication Data
Glover, David
What do pulleys and gears do? - 2nd Edition
621.8'3
A full catalogue record for this book is available from the British Library.

Acknowledgements
The publishers would like to thank the following for permission to reproduce photographs: Trevor Clifford pp1, 4, 5, 12, 14-19, 21; Collections/Keith Pritchard p9; Mary Evans Picture Library p10; Stockfile/ Steven Behr p20; TRIP/H Rogers p13; TSW/ Alastair Black p7; Zefa/Damm p6.

Cover photograph reproduced with permission of ImageState/ Stephen Jenkins.

The publishers would like to thank Angela Royston for her assistance in the preparation of this book.

Every effort has been made to contact copyright holders of any material reproduced in this book. Any omissions will be rectified in subsequent printings if notice is given to the publishers.

The paper used to print this book comes from sustainable resources.

Any words appearing in the text in bold, **like this**, are explained in the Glossary

The crank handle of this model is linked to the wheels by two gear wheels. The gear wheels have teeth around their edges. Some of the teeth on one wheel fit between some of the teeth on the other wheel. This is called **meshing**.

When one gear wheel turns, its teeth push the teeth on the other gear wheel. This makes the second gear wheel turn as well.

gear wheels

crank handle

FACT FILE **Different directions**

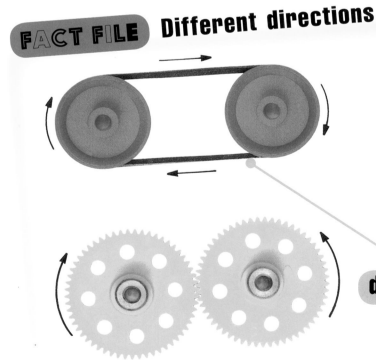

When two pulleys are linked by a drive belt, they go round in the same direction. Two gear wheels with meshed teeth go round in opposite directions.

drive belt

5

Up the pole

To make a flag go up a pole you pull down on the rope. As you pull down the flag goes up. How can a pull down make something go up?

If you look at the top of the pole you will see the answer. The rope goes over a pulley. The pulley changes the direction of the pull from down to up. So, as you pull down on the rope, the flag goes up.

Can you spot the pulleys on this yacht? Pulleys help sailors to raise the sails up the mast. The sailors pull down on ropes on the deck.

FACT FILE   The first pulleys

Who invented the pulley? Nobody knows, but the first pulleys were probably just smooth tree branches. Many people must have had the idea of throwing a rope over a tree branch to lift a heavy load high enough to keep it out of the reach of animals, or to put it on a cart.

Cranes and block and tackle

The hook on this crane is fixed to a pulley. A steel rope runs under the pulley, touching its underside. A powerful **motor** winds the rope up and down to raise the load. Other ropes and pulleys move the load to and fro along the arm of the crane. This arm is called the jib.

jib

steel rope

pulley

load

A block and tackle is a set of pulleys that work together. One person can lift a very heavy weight with a block and tackle. This boat was lifted out of the sea using a block and tackle.

FACT FILE **Making it easy**

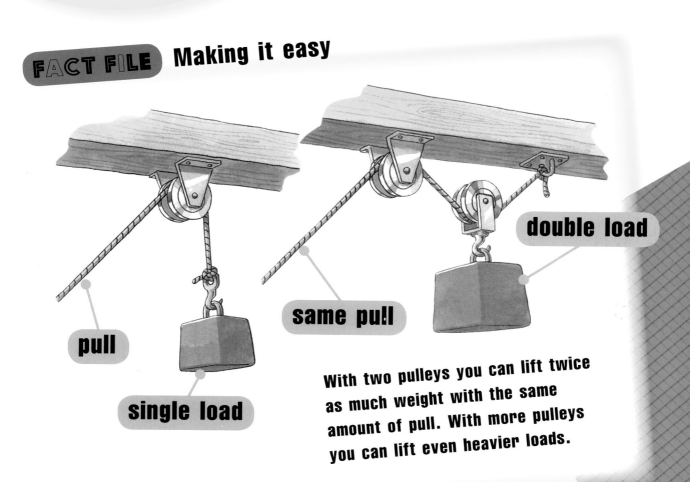

double load

pull

same pull

single load

With two pulleys you can lift twice as much weight with the same amount of pull. With more pulleys you can lift even heavier loads.

Drive belts

A **steam engine** drives this old-fashioned sewing machine. The engine is joined to the sewing machine by pulleys and a **drive belt**. The pulley on the machine is smaller than the pulley on the engine. This makes the sewing machine turn faster than the engine.

These pulley wheels are linked by a drive belt. Two wheels of the same size turn at the same speed.

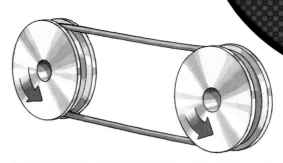

same size - same speed

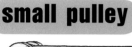

small pulley   large pulley

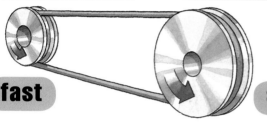

fast   slow

When the wheels are different sizes, the smaller wheel turns faster than the bigger one.

You can make pulley wheels turn in opposite directions by twisting and crossing over the drive belt.

crossed belt

pulley turns to left

pulley turns to right

FACT FILE Half the size, twice the speed

If one pulley is half the size of the other pulley, it turns round twice as quickly. This is because one turn of the large pulley makes the small pulley go round twice.

Power pulleys

Most rides at the fairground go round and round. Some of them are worked by **steam engines** with pulleys and drive belts. This is a model of an old steam engine. It has a **drive belt** that turns the back wheel to drive the engine along.

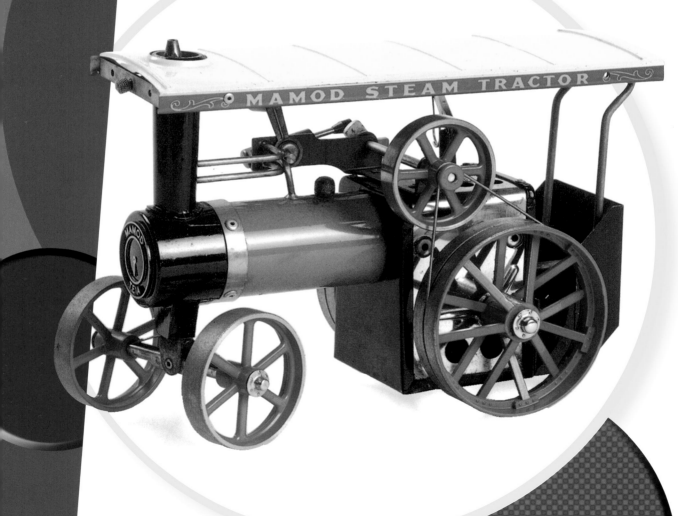

This machine crushes sugar cane to extract the juice. It has many moving parts. A steam engine drives it. Drive belts, pulleys, and gears make the parts go round.

FACT FILE   Be safe!

Drive belts and pulleys are very dangerous. You can trap your hair, your hands, or your clothes between the pulley and the belt. All modern pulleys are made safe with special safety guards.

Gear kits

You can learn about gears by making models with a gear kit. Flat, round gears are called **spur gears**. One spur gear can turn several other gears. This is called a **gear train**. The gears in the train go round in different directions. If the gears are different sizes, they go round at different speeds.

worm gear

gear train

A gear wheel which looks like a screw is called a worm gear. When a **worm gear** turns it makes a large spur gear go round very slowly.

Two gear wheels can be linked together with a chain that fits over their teeth. This is how the gears on a bicycle work. The chain makes both gear wheels go round in the same direction.

FACT FILE **Count the teeth**

These three gear wheels have 7 teeth, 10 teeth, and 14 teeth. Which two gears would you choose to make one gear turn twice as fast as the other? Look at page 24 to see if you were right.

Drills, whisks, and reels

When you turn the handle on this drill it makes the drill bit turn at high speed. The drill bit is held in the **chuck**. The handle is linked to the chuck by bevel gears. Bevel gears have sloping teeth. They change the direction in which things turn.

The gear wheel on the handle is much bigger than the gear wheels on the chuck. This means that the chuck goes round several times each time the handle turns once.

bevel gears

handle

chuck

This whisk has two blades. They are turned by gear wheels on either side of the big gear wheel on the handle. The blades turn in opposite directions, so everything mixes in very well.

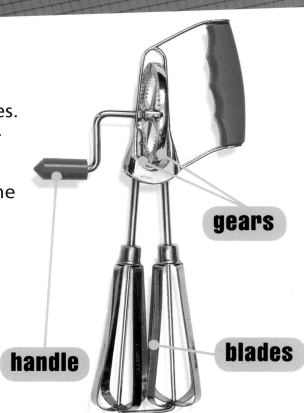

gears

handle

blades

FACT FILE Changing direction

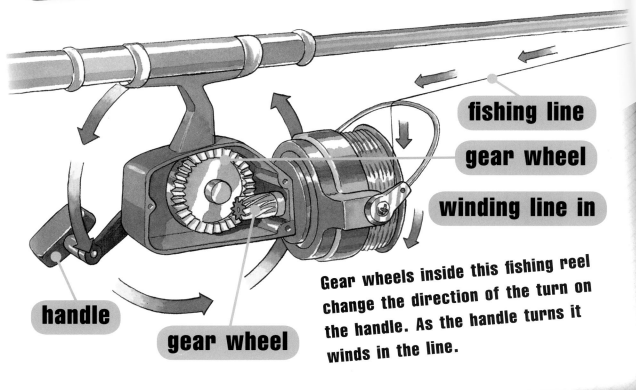

fishing line

gear wheel

winding line in

handle

gear wheel

Gear wheels inside this fishing reel change the direction of the turn on the handle. As the handle turns it winds in the line.

Clocks and watches

The three hands on a clock or watch go round at different speeds. The same **mechanism** turns them all. Each hand is linked to the mechanism by different gears.

During the time the hour hand turns one complete circle, the minute hand turns 12 times. Extra gears help the hour hand go more slowly than the minute hand.

hour hand

minute hand

second hand

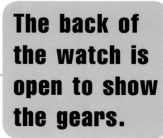

The back of the watch is open to show the gears.

Gears turn the hands of a cuckoo clock. They are powered by falling weights instead of a **motor**. Extra gears turn the parts that make the cuckoo pop out every hour.

FACT FILE Time flies!

The hour hand on a clock goes all the way round twice in 24 hours. The minute hand goes round 24 times, but the second hand goes round 1,440 times every 24 hours!

Mountain bikes

The chain on a mountain bike fits over the teeth on special gear wheels. These wheels are called **sprockets**. The chain carries the push on the pedals to the back wheel. This push turns the back wheel.

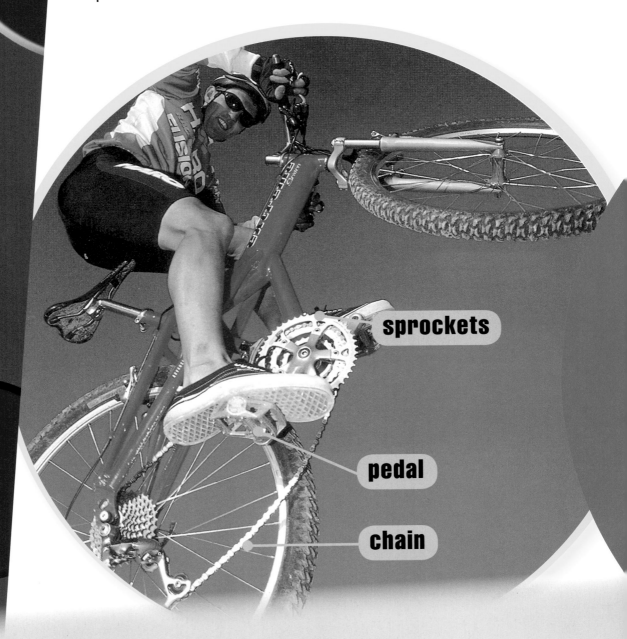

sprockets

pedal

chain

small sprockets

large sprockets

When you change gear on a bike, the chain moves between different sized sprockets on the back wheel. Large sprockets are easy gears for climbing hills. Small sprockets are hard gears for going fast along flat ground.

FACT FILE How many gears?

Some mountain bikes have 28 gears! Track racing bikes have only one gear.

Activities

A simple pulley

1. Tie a long piece of thread or string to a thick book.
2. Use the string to lift up the book.

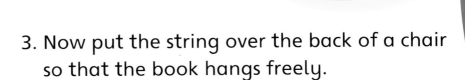

3. Now put the string over the back of a chair so that the book hangs freely.
4. Pull down on the string to lift up the book.
5. Which way of lifting the book is easier?

See pages 6–7 to find out why.

Gears in action

1. You will need an egg whisk like the one in the photo.
2. Slowly turn the handle and watch what happens.

3. The handle turns the big cog wheel.
4. The big cog wheel turns the two small cog wheels.
5. How many times does each beater go round when you turn the handle once?

See page 11 for an explanation.

Glossary

chuck the part on a drill that grips the different sized drill bits

drive belt loop of leather or rubber that links one pulley wheel to another

gear train series of gear wheels which carry turning movements from one part of a machine to another

mechanism the parts that move together to make a machine work

mesh when the teeth on two gear wheels fit together

motor a machine that uses electricity or fuels such as petrol or coal to make things move

sprockets the toothed wheels on the pedals and back wheel of a bicycle

spur gear flat circular gears with teeth around the edge

steam engine motor or engine which uses steam from boiling water to make things move

worm gear a gear like a screw with a spiral thread running around its surface

Index

The answer to the question on page 15 is:
the 7-toothed wheel goes twice as fast as the 14-toothed wheel.
Were you right?